RAMBLES IN

WHARFEDALE

HILLSIDE GUIDES

LONG DISTANCE WALKS

1 • THE WESTMORLAND WAY
2 • THE FURNESS WAY
3 • THE CUMBERLAND WAY
7 • CLEVELAND WAY COMPANION
9 • THE NORTH BOWLAND TRAVERSE
(by David Johnson)
16 • DALES WAY COMPANION

CIRCULAR WALKS - YORKSHIRE DALES

4 • WALKS IN WHARFEDALE
5 • WALKS IN NIDDERDALE
6 • WALKS IN THE CRAVEN DALES
8 • WALKS IN WENSLEYDALE
10 • WALKS IN THE WESTERN DALES
11 • WALKS IN SWALEDALE
20 • RAMBLES IN WHARFEDALE

CIRCULAR WALKS - NORTH YORK MOORS

13 • WESTERN - Cleveland/Hambleton Hills
14 • SOUTHERN - Rosedale/Farndale/Bransdale
15 • NORTHERN - Eskdale and the Coast

CIRCULAR WALKS - SOUTH PENNINES

12 • WALKS IN BRONTE COUNTRY
17 • WALKS IN CALDERDALE

HILLWALKING - THE LAKE DISTRICT

18 • OVER LAKELAND MOUNTAINS
19 • OVER LAKELAND FELLS

---

80 DALES WALKS
Published by Cordee, Leicester
An omnibus edition combining Books 4, 6, 8, 10, 11

RAMBLES
IN
WHARFEDALE

by

Paul Hannon

HILLSIDE PUBLICATIONS

HILLSIDE PUBLICATIONS
11 Nessfield Grove
Exley Head
Keighley
West Yorkshire
BD22 6NU

for Joseph

Page 1 illustration: Barden Bridge

ISBN 1 870141 12 1

Printed in Great Britain by
Carnmor Print and Design
95/97 London Road
Preston
Lancashire
PR1 4BA

INTRODUCTION

The subject of this book is the upper valley of the river Wharfe, from the boundary of the Yorkshire Dales National Park at Bolton Bridge to beyond Buckden: included is the quieter side-valley of Littondale. Wharfedale is the most popular valley in the Dales, this being attributable not least of all to its accessibility. The West Yorkshire cities of Leeds and Bradford and their surrounding towns are but a modest distance away, and on summer weekends the banks of the river see as many sun-worshippers as ramblers.

The Wharfe's name originates from the Celtic meaning 'swift water', and this lovely river races for almost 30 miles from Beckermonds to Bolton Bridge before a rather more sedate run to join the Ouse near Selby. At Beckermonds the Wharfe is formed by the confluence of Oughtershaw and Greenfield Becks, which have themselves already covered some distance from the lonely heights of Cam Fell.

The Wharfe's major tributary is the Skirfare, which flows through — and sometimes beneath — its own dale, Littondale to lose its identity near the famous landmark of Kilnsey Crag. Though Littondale has many characteristics of its big brother, it is separated by steep-sided fells and its seclusion gives it an intimate, possibly even greater charm.

North of Kilnsey the valley floors are dead flat and never more than half a mile wide, and at a very clearly-defined boundary the fells begin their majestic rise to numerous 2000-foot summits. At regular intervals their slopes are scored by crystal clear mountain becks which have a short-lived but very joyful journey. While the higher tops display the gritstone features of peat groughs and never-dry terrain, the lower slopes show off the ever-fascinating scars of gleaming limestone.

Lower down the dale meanwhile, gritstone dominates in the huge forms of Barden Moor and Fell. These extensive areas of rolling heather moorland face each other across the Wharfe, and together are valued grouse shooting country. Happily they are the subject of a negotiated access agreement with the landowner (the Duke of Devonshire's estates) and walkers are free to roam over the upland areas subject to various restrictions.

The main point is that the moors can be 'closed' on certain days when shooting takes place, though not Sundays. Although notices are posted at the access points (along with a list of all restrictions) disappointment can be avoided by ringing the estate office beforehand (Bolton Abbey 227). Also worth knowing—dogs are not allowed. Walks 1, 5 and 13 take advantage of this.

THE ROAD NETWORK

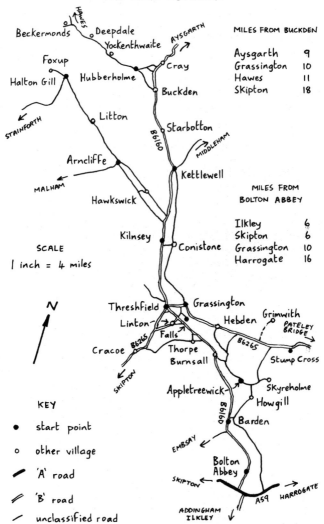

MILES FROM BUCKDEN

Aysgarth	9
Grassington	10
Hawes	11
Skipton	18

MILES FROM BOLTON ABBEY

Ilkley	6
Skipton	6
Grassington	10
Harrogate	16

SCALE
1 inch = 4 miles

KEY

- ● start point
- ○ other village
- ▰ 'A' road
- ⫽ 'B' road
- ⁄ unclassified road

The 16 walks described range in length from 2 to 12 miles, and the terrain similarly varies from riverside strolls to rather more strenuous moorland walking. All walks are circular, and with an average distance of 6½ miles are ideally suited to half-day rambles. Each walk is given its own chapter consisting of 'immediate impression' diagram, detailed narrative and strip-map and notes and illustrations of features of interest along the way.

Overleaf are listed the various facilities which can be found in the valley. There is ample accommodation in a variety of forms, including many of the inns. The vast majority of the villages have at least one licensed house, and virtually all are comfortable, well-kept establishments which lean heavily towards the visitor. The provision of food is as regular - and important- a feature as the availability of traditional beers.

Wharfedale has two conveniently sited youth hostels, with Linton serving the lower dale and Kettlewell covering the upper valley. Both also cater for walkers on the Dales Way, a long-distance route which runs the length of the dale, clinging largely to the riverbank before crossing into Dentdale. Bunk-barn accommodation is on the increase, and there are several camping sites in the valley.

The nearest railway station down the valley is at the cul-de-sac of Ilkley, though the station at Skipton is usually more accessible. It is also from Skipton that the dale is best served by bus, with the main service being to Grassington. In summer months some visitor-orientated services may well be found

Grassington is the largest centre with a good range of shops, but it is the thriving market town of Skipton that really serves the dale: the market can be found on the following days - Monday, Wednesday, Friday and Saturday. Early - closing days are Grassington, Thursday ; Skipton, Tuesday; Ilkley, Wednesday.

ORDNANCE SURVEY MAPS

Although the strip-maps illustrating each walk are sufficient to guide one safely around, they show nothing of the surrounding countryside. An Ordnance Survey map will provide the answer.

1:50,000 Landranger sheets 98, 99 and 104

1:25,000 Outdoor Leisure Maps 10 and 30 (Yorkshire Dales South and North/Central)

SOME USEFUL FACILITIES

	Accommodation	Inn	Car park	Bus service	Post office	other shop	WC	Payphone
Appletreewick	•	•		•				•
Arncliffe	•	•		•	•			•
Barden	•			•				•
Bolton Abbey	•	•	•	•	•	•	•	•
Burnsall	•	•	•	•	•	•	•	•
Conistone								•
Grassington	•	•	•	•	•	•	•	•
Grimwith Reservoir			•				•	
Halton Gill								•
Howgill	•			•		•		•
Hubberholme	•	•						
Kettlewell	•	•	•	•	•	•	•	•
Kilnsey	•	•		•				
Linton Falls			•				•	
Skyreholme	•							•
Starbotton	•	•		•				•
Stump Cross Caverns			•	•		•	•	
Threshfield	•	•		•	•	•		•

A rough guide only!

8

SOME USEFUL ADDRESSES

Ramblers' Association
1/5 Wandsworth Road, London SW8 2XX
Tel. 071-582 6878

Youth Hostels Association
Trevelyan House, St. Albans, Herts. AL1 2DY
Tel. St. Albans (0727) 55215

Yorkshire Dales National Park
Office and Information Centre
Colvend, Hebden Road, Grassington,
Skipton, North Yorkshire BD23 5LB
Tel. Grassington (0756) 752748

Ilkley Tourist Information
Station Road, Ilkley
Tel. Ilkley (0943) 602319

Skipton Tourist Information
Victoria Square, Skipton
Tel. Skipton (0756) 792809

Yorkshire and Humberside Tourist Board
312 Tadcaster Road, York YO2 2HF
Tel. York (0904) 707961

Yorkshire Dales Society
152 Main Street, Addingham, Ilkley,
West Yorkshire LS29 0LY

Keighley and District Travel
Bus Station, Townfieldgate, Keighley
Tel. Keighley (0535) 603284

Bolton Abbey Estate Office
(Barden Moor and Fell access areas)
Tel. Bolton Abbey (075671) 227

THE WALKS

Listed below are the 16 walks described, the walk number being the key to easy location in the guide

THE WALKS

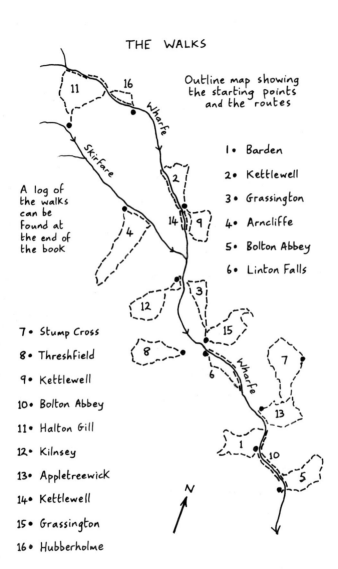

Outline map showing
the starting points
and the routes

1 • Barden

2 • Kettlewell

3 • Grassington

4 • Arncliffe

5 • Bolton Abbey

6 • Linton Falls

A log of
the walks
can be
found at
the end of
the book

7 • Stump Cross

8 • Threshfield

9 • Kettlewell

10 • Bolton Abbey

11 • Halton Gill

12 • Kilnsey

13 • Appletreewick

14 • Kettlewell

15 • Grassington

16 • Hubberholme

WALK 1

8 miles

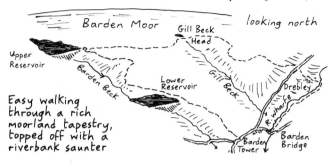

OVER BARDEN MOOR

from Barden

Easy walking through a rich moorland tapestry, topped off with a riverbank saunter

There is a parking area by the river at Barden Bridge, and in the season the adjacent field is opened up.

NOTE BEFORE STARTING: *The walk crosses the Wharfe by stepping stones at Drebley, a potential impasse if the river is high or one's confidence is low. They are however, in very good condition.*

■ The entire moorland section of the walk is on the Barden Moor access area: see the notes at the foot of page 5.

THE WALK (at last)

From Barden Bridge take the road climbing steeply to the tower, and turn left along the main road just as far as the Skipton turning. Only yards up it, escape by a gate on the right, from where a stony track heads off across the moor. Arriving above the dam of Lower Barden Reservoir, the track runs on past its head before starting a climb to the dam of its higher neighbour.

After a potter about, return the few yards to a junction where a footpath sign to Burnsall invites a much pleasanter - particularly on the feet- ramble on a traditional moorland track. It maintains a near-level course for some time, contouring splendidly round to an attractive little dam. Across its modest embankment a crossroads is reached : turn right on a track through thick heather, running along to join a similar track by some grouse butts. Once again going right, this one drops down to a crossroads by another row of butts, the right-hand arm being the return of the short-cut path shown on the map.

At this junction turn left, the broad track soon becoming delightful underfoot as it runs along towards the moor-edge. The final grassy Knoll is a good place to take stock, with a marvellous prospect across the valley to the deep bowl of the Appletreewick-Skyreholme area. Below us the track drops down to the head of a green lane, which descends in no-nonsense fashion to the Burnsall road.

Almost opposite, the access road to Drebley provides immediate escape as it resumes our fall to the river. After the first building turn into the farmyard on the left, continuing straight through to emerge on a level, green track. It crosses a field, then part-way through the next one turn down to a gateway at the very bottom. Below, the Wharfe's bank is gained at the stepping stones.

Moving swiftly to the opposite bank (in the text, at least) the final stage of the walk traces a very beautiful and tranquil reach of the Wharfe downstream. The path concludes by rising to the road just short of Barden Bridge, and a final 'unofficial' short-lived path springs up to parallel the road, if so required.

Barden Tower was built as a hunting lodge by the powerful Cliffords of Skipton Castle, and it boasted two famous residents from that family. Henry the 'Shepherd Lord' came in 1485, being raised in the Cumbrian fells until the Wars of the Roses ended. Up to his death in 1523 he preferred Barden's peace and the company of the canons of Bolton to Skipton's splendour. He also had the adjacent chapel built.

The redoubtable Lady Anne had the Tower restored in 1659 and spent much of her final years here, a stone tablet on an exterior wall surviving to confirm her work. In 1676 she died, last of the Cliffords, and the long process of decay began.

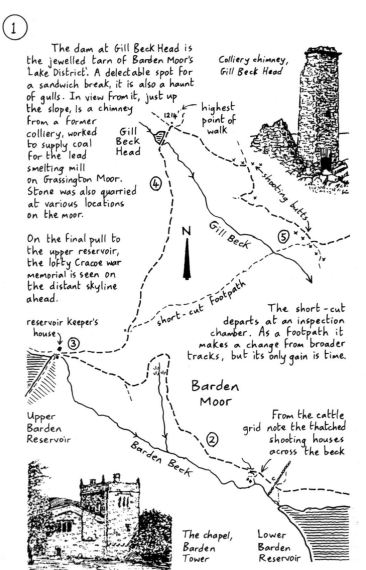

The dam at Gill Beck Head is the dam's 'Lake District'. A delectable spot for a sandwich break, it is also a haunt of gulls. In view from it, just up the slope, is a chimney from a former colliery, worked to supply coal for the lead smelting mill on Grassington Moor. Stone was also quarried at various locations on the moor.

On the final pull to the upper reservoir, the lofty Cracoe war memorial is seen on the distant skyline ahead.

Colliery chimney, Gill Beck Head

1214' highest point of walk

Gill Beck Head

shooting butts

④

Gill Beck

⑤

N

short-cut Footpath

The short-cut departs at an inspection chamber. As a footpath it makes a change from broader tracks, but its only gain is time.

reservoir keeper's house

③

Barden Moor

Upper Barden Reservoir

From the cattle grid note the thatched shooting houses across the beck

Barden Beck

②

The chapel, Barden Tower

Lower Barden Reservoir

Drebley's stepping stones display much more character than the concrete blocks encountered on Walk 14, and unlike that walk, a refusal will incur three penalty points and more importantly retraced steps, for there is no path in either direction on Drebley's bank of the Wharfe. Those of a nervous disposition will find no solace in the knowledge that a footbridge existed here a number of decades ago. Back on the east bank is a barn that was formerly Hough Mill, restored by none other than Lady Anne Clifford, in 1657.

Drebley itself is a timeless farming community that was once a forest lodge.

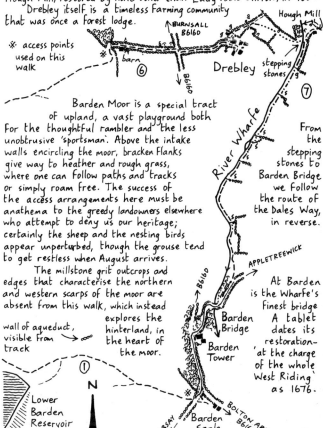

✳ access points used on this walk

Barden Moor is a special tract of upland, a vast playground both for the thoughtful rambler and the less unobtrusive 'sportsman'. Above the intake walls encircling the moor, bracken flanks give way to heather and rough grass, where one can follow paths and tracks or simply roam free. The success of the access arrangements here must be anathema to the greedy landowners elsewhere who attempt to deny us our heritage; certainly the sheep and the nesting birds appear unperturbed, though the grouse tend to get restless when August arrives.

The millstone grit outcrops and edges that characterise the northern and western scarps of the moor are absent from this walk, which instead explores the hinterland, in the heart of the moor.

wall of aqueduct, visible from track

Lower Barden Reservoir

N

From the stepping stones to Barden Bridge we follow the route of the Dales Way, in reverse.

At Barden is the Wharfe's finest bridge. A tablet dates its restoration 'at the charge of the whole West Riding' as 1676.

Hough Mill

BURNSALL B6160

barn ⑥

B6160

Drebley

stepping stones

⑦

River Wharfe

APPLETREEWICK

B6160

Barden Bridge

Barden Tower

Barden Scale

EMBSAY

BOLTON ABBEY B6160

15

WALK 2

5¾ miles

CAM HEAD AND STARBOTTON

from Kettlewell

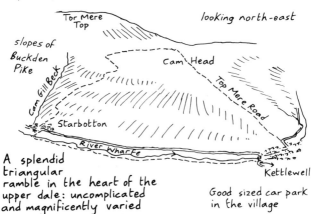

looking north-east

A splendid
triangular
ramble in the heart of the
upper dale: uncomplicated
and magnificently varied

Good sized car park
in the village

THE WALK

Leave the main road through the village by way of the side-road heading off opposite the Racehorses Hotel. Cross straight over at the crossroads by the post office shop (signposted Leyburn) and the road soon swings left to climb out of the village. Within a minute it turns sharply right, and here we leave it by continuing up the unsurfaced walled lane straight ahead. This is Top Mere Road, which after a relatively steep start - excuse to pause to admire the fine retrospective view down Wharfedale - soon eases out to become an outstanding green lane: all that is required is to tread its caressing surface. Eventually all enclosing walls will be shrugged off, and the track rises across the fell to arrive at a cairn and guidepost at Cam Head.

Here at the summit of the walk we encounter equally inviting Starbotton Road, and after a deserved sojourn, go left along this new green road for a brief level spell. After a second intervening wall, the way begins an emphatic descent to Starbotton, now as Starbotton Cam Road. As the valley floor is neared, steepening zigzags bear down on the huddled roofs of the village. A stony finish leads onto a back lane, with several options for reaching the main road.

If seeking the hostelry bear to the right, otherwise turn along to the Kettlewell end of the village. Here a walled track heads away, running along to a footbridge across the Wharfe. Turn downstream on the opposite bank, and all is now plain sailing. For the most part the path - along with its innumerable stiles - remains near the river and easy to follow: there are just a couple of instances where it cuts out lazy meanderings, these points being less than obvious from this direction.

All in good time the houses of Kettlewell come into sight, though the path must adhere to the river to arrive at the road bridge at the main entrance to the village.

Looking down the valley (over Kettlewell) from the Top Mere Road

The regular appendage of 'road' names to the various green tracks of this walk is a sign of their importance in times past. Today classic walkers' highways, they originally served more functional tasks, and both the contrasting styles of the Top Mere and Starbotton Cam Roads would be used to reach peat grounds and small-scale lead workings. Their well-laid courses were designed for easy descent with the spoils. The road out of Starbotton was, in addition, on a packhorse route and drove road between Coverdale and Malham.

Starbotton sits midway between two larger and better known neighbours, Kettlewell and Buckden. Though the valley road passes through, few visitors halt here other than for refreshment at the attractive, whitewashed inn. Off the main road however are some charming corners, with 17th century cottages and a small Quaker burial ground hidden away.

Starbotton nestles comfortably under Buckden Pike, and like its neighbours stands above the river on its swift-flowing beck, which caused disastrous flooding in a deluge in 1686.

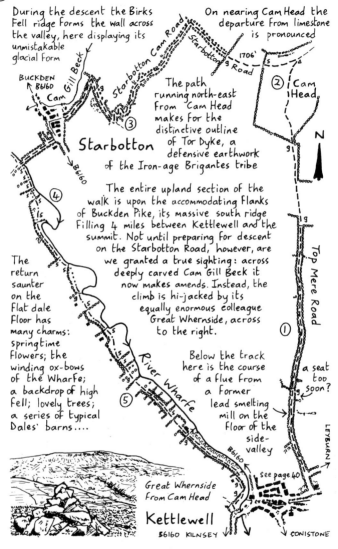

During the descent the Birks Fell ridge forms the wall across the valley, here displaying its unmistakable glacial form

On nearing Cam Head the departure from limestone is pronounced

1706'

BUCKDEN ↑ B6160
Cam

Starbotton Cam Road

Starbotton Road

③

Starbotton

② Cam Head

N

The path running north-east from Cam Head makes for the distinctive outline of Tor Dyke, a defensive earthwork of the Iron-age Brigantes tribe

B6160

④

The entire upland section of the walk is upon the accommodating flanks of Buckden Pike, its massive south ridge filling 4 miles between Kettlewell and the summit. Not until preparing for descent on the Starbotton Road, however, are we granted a true sighting: across deeply carved Cam Gill Beck it now makes amends. Instead, the climb is hi-jacked by its equally enormous colleague Great Whernside, across to the right.

Top Mere Road

The return saunter on the flat dale floor has many charms: springtime flowers; the winding ox-bows of the Wharfe; a backdrop of high fell; lovely trees; a series of typical Dales' barns....

River Wharfe

⑤

①

Below the track here is the course of a flue from a former lead smelting mill on the floor of the side-valley

a seat too soon?

LEYBURN

B6160

See page 40

Great Whernside from Cam Head

Kettlewell

B6160 KILNSEY ↓

↓ CONISTONE

WALK 3

7 miles

from Grassington

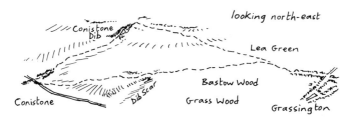

looking north-east

Conistone Dib — Lea Green — Bastow Wood — Grass Wood — Conistone — Dib Scar — Grassington

Easy walking on lush turf, with limestone features in abundance

Most suitable car park is the Town Hall/Institute one, at the very top of Main Street. Alternatively, use the main Hebden Road car park.

THE WALK

From the cobbled square head up the main street past the Devonshire Arms, and at the crossroads by the Town Hall go left along Church Street. When it eventually turns sharply to the left at Town Head, turn into the farmyard on the right. Skirt round to the right of the main buildings to a gate after the last building, then follow the right-hand wall away. At the end take the central of three gates and bear left to a painfully narrow gapstile at the far end. In the next enclosure curve to the left to a stile in the far wall, behind which a further stile admits to the great expanse of Lea Green.

After crossing a wider track, a gentle rise leads up to join another track heading our way. A little further on a sketchy left fork is ignored, and at the brow a near-parallel wall is seen to the right. Our path refuses to fully join it until beyond a limestone pavement, when we cross to a stile just short of the corner. Head away to a gate beyond an island outcrop and then rise to a stile, continuing up past further outcrops to a huge kiln and a stile just over the brow. Level pastures then precede a short pull to the head of Conistone Dib.

At the very head of the ravine leave the path for a stile on the left, and turn immediately down to a stile where a wall abuts onto a cliff. The way to Conistone is henceforward infallible, descending roughly at first before a saunter through the dry valley. Near the foot the walls of rock close in again to form the remarkable gorge of Gurling Trough, through which arrival in Conistone seems very sudden.

On passing through the green to join the road, keep left along the back road to Grassington, and before the last house on the left turn up a rough track. This rises pleasantly through several pastures towards the attractive Grass and Bastow Woods directly ahead. After passing through identical corners in walls the walk's third spectacular moment reveals itself, as the ravine of Dib Scar appears at one's feet.

The path takes evasive action by swinging left to run along the rim of the dry valley. At its head a stile takes us over the wall and up the slope behind to pass through a gap in the next parallel wall. Heading directly away, a stile by a gateway is used to cross the left-hand wall, which is then followed away to the right. We are now back on the pastures of Lea Green, and on this occasion we have the delights of Bastow Wood just over the wall.

Eventually the wall is forsaken by trending left on a green track, which descends steadily to intersect the outward route just above the stile onto Lea Green. Here leave the track to drop down to the stile to retrace steps into Grassington.

Winter above Dib Scar: the return path from the outward path on Lea Green

Bastow Wood, with its lower neighbour Grass Wood, is rich in botanic interest in addition to its more obvious wooded charm.

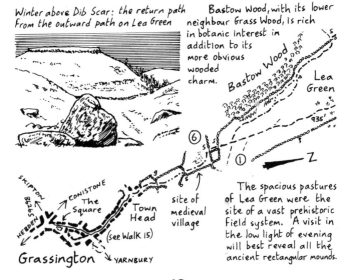

The spacious pastures of Lea Green were the site of a vast prehistoric field system. A visit in the low light of evening will best reveal all the ancient rectangular mounds.

Conistone is an attractive, greystone little village well away from the main road, which heads updale half a mile distant, across the river at Kilnsey. Even from this distance the famous crag retains its grandeur. Every block of stone in Conistone's cottages matches the natural landscape of the village's hinterland. Though restored a century ago, the hidden church retains some Norman work.

↑KILNSEY

R. Wharfe

KETTLEWELL

Conistone

GRASSINGTON←

④

g

Gurling Trough

Conistone Dib is a classic example of a dry limestone valley, narrowing to slender gorges at either end. Gurling Trough is a miniature Gordale, while the Dib head is a slim ravine.

←Z

Early on the return we have a good view back over Conistone's rooftops to the dark shadow of Kilnsey Crag

Dib Scar

⑤

Conistone Dib

③

1050'

Note the size of the blocks in this solid Kiln↘

The short-cut branching off here should only be used in dire emergency

↖dewpond

②

As far as Conistone Dib we follow the Dales Way having a rare break from the river

Dib Scar - or simply the Dib - is another dry limestone gorge, enhanced by a backdrop of woodland, and of sufficient cragginess to have attracted climbers. Above it stands an absolute gem of a sloping pavement.

Updale from the pavement

WALK 4 | MALHAM TARN AND THE MONK'S ROAD

12 miles | from Arncliffe

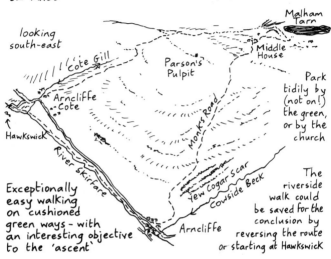

looking
south-east

Malham Tarn

Cote Gill

Parson's
Pulpit

Middle
House

Arncliffe
Cote

Hawkswick

River Skirfare

Monks Road

Park
tidily by
(not on!)
the green,
or by the
church

Yew Cogar Scar

Cowside Beck

Exceptionally
easy walking
on cushioned
green ways - with
an interesting objective
to the 'ascent'

Arncliffe

The
riverside
walk could
be saved for the
conclusion by
reversing the route
or starting at Hawkswick

THE WALK

From the green cross to the up-dale road, but leave
it almost at once for a drive on the right immediately before
the church. Just to the right of a barn we emerge into a
field, and an uncomplicated downstream stroll ensues. The path
is generally clear, and little description is needed other than
keeping an eye on the map and the waymarks. Initially in
the company of the Skirfare, the path keeps its distance
for the middle section before returning to its bank to reach
Hawkswick Footbridge.

Without crossing it, turn up the short byway onto a
lane. This narrowest of roads climbs up to the right to join
the main Littondale road, which is followed a short distance
to the right. The second of near-parallel drives should be
taken to rise to the farm at Arncliffe Cote. A track takes
over past the buildings to soon emerge onto the grassy fell.

After a zigzag it commences a long, very gradual
climb high above the ravine of Cote Gill across to the left.
The pastures are long and the going easy as the higher

reaches of the gill and surrounding uplands are penetrated on a resplendant track on velvet turf. A hint of steepness is encountered before a brief foray with real 'Fell-like' terrain on the highest point, Lee Gate High Mark. As the track winds down through the extensive pasture of Great Close, there will be little awareness yet that we are on the threshold of the many delights of the Malham district. In the corner of the pasture an exhuberant stream is forded and a final pasture crossed to meet Mastiles Lane at Street Gate.

Here turn right to a crossroads, forsaking the tarmac road for the unsurfaced drive on the right, which heads for Malham Tarn House. Beyond a gate it enters the environs of Malham Tarn itself, running near the shore and approaching the wooded grounds of the house. Without entering the trees, leave the drive and double back up to the right on a path rising to the saddle between Highfolds (left) and Great Close Hill: this is the Monk's Road, which in due course will return us to Arncliffe.

Beyond the gap the path runs along towards Middle House Farm, but beyond an intervening fence we can slant steadily left, rising to meet a track climbing from the Farm. Beyond a stile continue only a minute further through the limestone outcrops, then fork right on a path that joins a wall. After the cluster of barns at Old Middle House, the path crosses a collapsed wall to a guidepost, to bear right on the clearer Arncliffe path.

Little further description is needed as the path runs on through outcrops, pavements and a miscellany of stiles. In time the path drops a little to run along the well-defined crest of Yew Cogar Scar. As the scars recede the path gets to grips with the descent to Arncliffe, clearly in view on the dale floor.

A delightful little lane is joined to lead into the village, rather handily adjacent to the Falcon Inn on the green.

Tarn House was built as a shooting lodge for Lord Ribblesdale in the late 18th century, and later improved into a country house in an unusually bleak situation by the Morrisons. It has long been used as a Field studies centre.

Arncliffe is one of the most attractive yet least spoilt villages in the Dales, and is regarded as the 'capital' of Littondale. A variety of characterful greystone houses stand back in relaxed manner from a spacious green. The unpretentious inn maintains this mood, and is in fact the only hostelry in the area to serve its ale in that unrivalled fashion, directly from the barrel.

Out of sight of the green is the church of St. Oswald, which has found its own niche, embowered in trees in a truly beautiful riverside setting. Though largely rebuilt last century, the solid tower dates back 500 years. Inside is a list of the Littondale men who marched off to fight at Flodden Field in 1513.

Across the shapely bridge, the house at Bridge End played host to Charles Kingsley during his 'Water Babies' period.

A National Trust property, Malham Tarn stands at 1230' in limestone country due to a layer of Silurian slate. Trout fishing dates back to monastic times, while Kingsley drew inspiration here. The tarn and adjacent mosses are an important nature reserve.

The Monk's Road leaves no doubt as to its original patrons, followed by packhorses and now walkers, who are treated to ever-expanding vistas over the scars to Littondale entrenched between Darnbrook and Birks Fells.

Sheep farming at Middle House dates from Norse times, before passing into the hands of Fountains Abbey.

Great Close was the setting, 200 years ago, for the biggest cattle fairs in the north

The summit of the walk reveals a sweeping prospect over Craven to that great landmark Pendle Hill, in Lancashire

A section of Mastiles Lane (see Walk 12) appears from above Gordale Beck

Dew Bottoms

Clowder

Monk's Road

Old Middle House (restored) 1990

Middle House Farm

limekiln

1673

Lee Gate High Mark

Malham Moor

Great Close

Gordale Beck

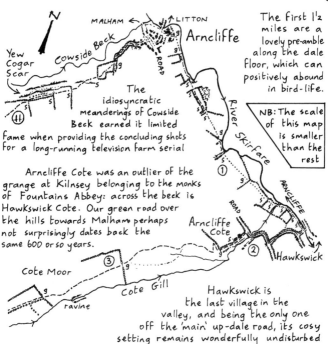

The first 1½ miles are a lovely pre-amble along the dale floor, which can positively abound in bird-life.

NB: The scale of this map is smaller than the rest

The idiosyncratic meanderings of Cowside Beck earned it limited fame when providing the concluding shots for a long-running television farm serial

Arncliffe Cote was an outlier of the grange at Kilnsey belonging to the monks of Fountains Abbey: across the beck is Hawkswick Cote. Our green road over the hills towards Malham perhaps not surprisingly dates back the same 600 or so years.

Hawkswick is the last village in the valley, and being the only one off the 'main' up-dale road, its cosy setting remains wonderfully undisturbed

Though hardly demanding rest-stops, the climb by often-dry Cote Gill should be broken to enjoy increasing vistas back over Littondale

Old Cote Moor and Great Whernside from Cote Gill

WALK 5

6 miles

HAZLEWOOD MOOR AND STORITHS

from Bolton Abbey

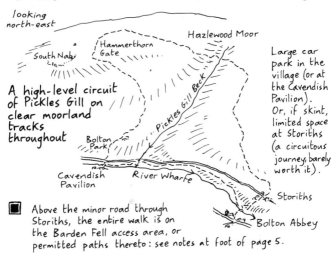

looking north-east

A high-level circuit of Pickles Gill on clear moorland tracks throughout

Large car park in the village (or at the Cavendish Pavilion). Or, if skint, limited space at Storiths (a circuitous journey, barely worth it).

◼ Above the minor road through Storiths, the entire walk is on the Barden Fell access area, or permitted paths thereto: see notes at foot of page 5.

THE WALK

Leave the road through Bolton Abbey by the famous 'Hole in the Wall' by the post office, and descend with the crowds to the ever lovely environs of the priory ruins. A look round might be better enjoyed at the end of the walk, so for now cross the wooden footbridge and turn upstream. Almost at once the main path bears right to gently scale the hillside: at the first opportunity take the branch doubling back up to the right to the top of the wood. Here a narrow, deeply inurned snicket whisks us away from the Bolton Abbey scene, climbing to a farm and then up its road to meet the minor road through Storiths.

Across the road is the pocket moor of Storiths Crag, and on turning a short distance up to the right, a stony drive heads off by the wall-side. This is the start of an extended route onto the Barden Fell access area, though within only a couple of minutes we will be on open moor. Approaching Town End Farm, bear right onto the moor, and a little further bear right at a fork for the track to begin a steady pull towards the heights.

As height is gained the intake wall returns, and at another fork our route takes the initially less appealing way to the right. This green track soon perks up, to head straight on as a similar track comes in from the right. Down to the left are a handful of fields encircling Intake Farm, and when a track climbs from it to briefly join us, take no notice as it quickly resumes its climb to the right. Our route now begins a cautious drop towards Pickles Gill Beck, reaching the stream at a sheepfold in a setting that begs a refreshment halt.

The path makes a short, steep climb from the fold before easing out to undulate along to a junction. Here we go down to the left to arrive at Hammerthorn Gate. On the knoll to the right an Ordnance column set well back from South Nab may tempt a detour before continuing down the stony track. After the next gate it descends through green pastures to Bolton Park, and to the right of the buildings its drive leads down to the Storiths – Barden road.

Cross straight over to the wooden bridge over the Wharfe, and if not visiting the Cavendish Pavilion across it, take the riverbank path downstream. At the far end of the pasture we are deflected onto the road to negotiate Pickles Beck, with a hidden footbridge upstream of the ford. On the other side two paths plunge into the riverside woods: both lead unfailingly back to the priory footbridge, though the higher one offers a more rewarding trek.

The snicket to Storiths   — Bolton Abbey —   Hole in the Wall

27

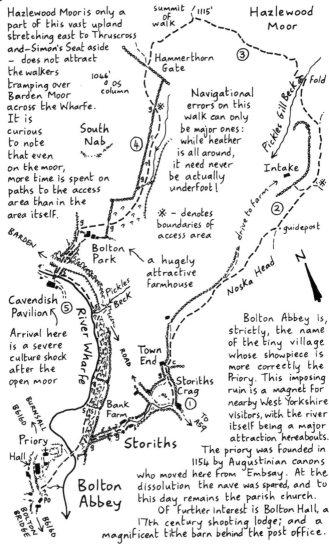

Hazlewood Moor is only a part of this vast upland stretching east to Thruscross and—Simon's Seat aside—does not attract the walkers tramping over Barden Moor across the Wharfe. It is curious to note that even on the moor, more time is spent on paths to the access area than in the area itself.

summit of walk / 1115'

Hazlewood Moor

Hammerthorn Gate

③

Pickles Gill Beck

Fold

1046' Ø OS column

South Nab

④

Navigational errors on this walk can only be major ones: while heather is all around, it need never be actually underfoot!

Intake

drive to farm →

②

※ – denotes boundaries of access area

BARDEN

Bolton Park

← a hugely attractive farmhouse

guidepost

Noska Head

N

Pickles Beck

Cavendish Pavilion ⑤

Arrival here is a severe culture shock after the open moor

River Wharfe

ROAD

Town End

Storiths Crag

①

TO A59

Bolton Abbey is, strictly, the name of the tiny village whose showpiece is more correctly the Priory. This imposing ruin is a magnet for nearby West Yorkshire visitors, with the river itself being a major attraction hereabouts.

BURNSALL B6160

Bank Farm

Storiths

Priory Hall

Bolton Abbey

PO

BOLTON BRIDGE B6160

The priory was founded in 1154 by Augustinian canons who moved here from Embsay. At the dissolution the nave was spared, and to this day remains the parish church.

Of further interest is Bolton Hall, a 17th century shooting lodge; and a magnificent tithe barn behind the post office.

WALK 6 | BURNSALL AND THE WHARFE

6¼ miles   from Linton Falls

An undemanding walk clinging tightly to the river after
an outward leg offering fine Wharfedale views

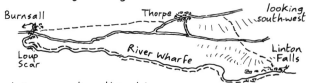

Good size car park on the cul de sac
road to Linton Church. Grassington's main car park is equally
accessible, just up the snicket from Linton Falls.
Burnsall, of course, makes an alternative starting point.

THE WALK

From the car park head along the road towards
the church, but if saving its charm for the end of the
walk, turn up a short enclosed way before a house on
the right. At the end (ignoring another way branching
off it) a meadow is entered, and crossed to a stile on
the left of the barn ahead. From it rise diagonally up
above the steeper drop, to arrive at a stile in the
distant facing wall. Two slender fields then precede
emergence onto the Burnsall road.

Turn right a few yards to a gate opposite
and rise half-left to a gate in a fence. Slightly left
again takes us to an elusive hand-gate, behind which
a narrow green snicket wends its way up to join the
similarly narrow Thorpe Lane. Go left into the hamlet
and at the tree-shrouded green bear left past the last
of the buildings. Just a little further, leave the road
by a rough lane on the right: at its early demise
drop down through a slender field to an intervening
fence and down again to a stile by a trickling stream.
The way rises away in a virtual straight line, across
a trio of fields to reach the unsurfaced Badger Lane.

A stile opposite resumes the fields' crossing, and
after dropping down the first field a direct course for
Burnsall is set, its church tower a useful guide. More
guidance is provided by a tightly-bunched series of stiles,

designed to test one's agility in addition to deferring arrival in Burnsall. The village is entered by way of a back yard, then turning right along the street into the centre.

Join the Wharfe by turning down between the Red Lion and the bridge, and follow a hugely popular path upstream. It soon sees the back of the village, passing below the church and along to a knoll above the gorge of Loup Scar. In these spectacular environs the path drops back down to the river to run through lovely wooded surroundings to the suspension bridge below Hebden.

On the opposite bank this uncomplicated leg of the walk resumes, through a deeply inurned reach of the Wharfe. On emerging, a loop in the river is cut out by striking across a large pasture to the right of the tree-masked sewage works. At its access road turn right along it, away from the river and up past a fish farm. As the track climbs through a bend, take a stile on the left to regain the Wharfe's bank opposite Linton Church. A couple of fields further and the footbridge at Linton Falls leads to a snicket back onto the road near the car park.

The Tin Bridge, Linton Falls

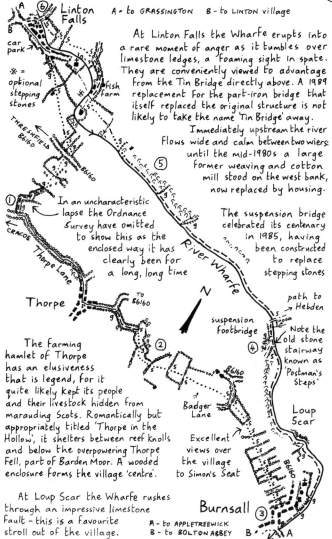

A Linton Falls ⑥

A - to GRASSINGTON   B - to LINTON village

B
car park ↗

☀ = optional stepping stones

Fish farm

THRESHFIELD B6160

B6160

① In an uncharacteristic lapse the Ordnance Survey have omitted to show this as the enclosed way it has clearly been for a long, long time

CRACOE Thorpe Lane

River Wharfe

⑤

Thorpe

TO B6160

N

②

The farming hamlet of Thorpe has an elusiveness that is legend, for it quite likely kept its people and their livestock hidden from marauding Scots. Romantically but appropriately titled 'Thorpe in the Hollow', it shelters between reef knolls and below the overpowering Thorpe Fell, part of Barden Moor. A wooded enclosure forms the village 'centre'.

Badger Lane

B6160

Excellent views over the village to Simon's Seat

path to Hebden

suspension footbridge

Note the old stone stairway known as 'Postman's Steps'

④

Loup Scar

At Loup Scar the Wharfe rushes through an impressive limestone fault – this is a favourite stroll out of the village.

Burnsall

③

B6160

A - to APPLETREEWICK
B - to BOLTON ABBEY   B ↙ ↓ A

At Linton Falls the Wharfe erupts into a rare moment of anger as it tumbles over limestone ledges, a foaming sight in spate. They are conveniently viewed to advantage from the Tin Bridge directly above. A 1989 replacement for the part-iron bridge that itself replaced the original structure is not likely to take the name 'Tin Bridge' away. Immediately upstream the river flows wide and calm between two weirs: until the mid-1980s a large former weaving and cotton mill stood on the west bank, now replaced by housing.

The suspension bridge celebrated its centenary in 1985, having been constructed to replace stepping stones

Burnsall's setting is one of near-perfection, with bridge, green- and maypole- church, inn and cottages fusing into an unforgettable Wharfedale scene. The church is just outside the centre, but worth a short walk up the road past the post office. It dates largely from the 15th century, and has an inscribed Norman font - note also the functional lych-gate. Alongside is the lovely school, founded in 1602 as one of the earliest grammar schools.

Top:
Loup Scar

Above:
St. Wilfrid's

Left:
the bridge from the green

WALK 7

7½ miles

TROLLERS GILL AND GRIMWITH
from Stump Cross

looking
north-east

Grimwith Reservoir

Nursery Knot

Grimwith Fell

Dry Gill

Stump Cross Caverns

Dibble's Bridge

Trollers Gill

Parceval Hall

Skyreholme

A fascinatingly varied trek along a series of old tracks. Trollers Gill is only one of many natural features

Start from a large lay-by below the steep bend in the road just beneath Stump Cross Caverns (which also has a large car park).
Alternative start: Water Authority car park, Grimwith Reservoir.

THE WALK

At the foot of the steep pull to the Caverns, a path leaves the road at a small pocket of open ground. After a stile it quickly shakes off its accompanying wall and rises to the foot of prominent Nursery Knot. The path passes behind the outcrop, but few will resist a closer look. At the wall corner behind, two adjacent stiles can be taken in tandem without touching the ground before a line of stakes point the way to Grimwith Reservoir. These stakes maintain the route down through several rough enclosures before crossing two fields to the reservoir road.

Head left along this unsurfaced road round the water, and beyond a barn-like structure a 'hard' path breaks off the hard road to run nearer the shore before climbing back to it. A little further along, the road runs into the car park: turn up the drive between toilets and houses, and from the gate above a splendid moorland track runs along to the Pateley Bridge road.

Cross straight over onto a green lane, soon losing an enclosing wall to run an idyllic course to join New Road on a bend. Go left the few yards to a stile from where an unclear path bears half-left: soon it drops to a hollow on the left, passing Hell Hole to meet a wide track. Turn right, noting the location of Trollers Gill across the grassy neck supporting Middle Hill. Although there is no definitive path, walkers regularly cross the brow to the stile above the ravine, then enjoying a spectacular walk through to the entrance and on to the foot of Middle Hill.

Here our right-of-way is met after its pleasant descent of the mine road and past the former workings. United again, the charming green path runs above the bank of Skyreholme Beck, eventually emerging on the drive to Parceval Hall. Cross the bridge and from a stile in the yard-corner head across the field with a wall. At the second gateway enter a field on the right to drop diagonally to a gate by the road at Skyreholme.

Turn left for a long, steady pull before the road finally loses its surface. Keep left at a fork a little further on, and continue over the brow on the welcoming green surface of Black Hill Road. In time it drops down towards Dry Gill to join the Pateley Bridge road just down to the left of the starting point.

HEBDEN

B6265

③ Fancarl Crag

New Road → DRY GILL

APPLETREEWICK

old lead mine

④

old dam (burst 1899)

Middle Hill

Hell Hole – a black slit forms the entrance

Trollers Gill

Skyreholme Beck

Parceval ↙Hall

Parceval – probably the grandest house in upper Wharfedale, dating back to Elizabethan times and now a diocesan retreat centre. The gardens and woodland are open to view, Easter to October.

APPLETREEWICK ←

⑤ Skyreholme

Skyreholme Bank

⑥ Simon's Seat dominates the scene hereabouts

Trollers Gill is a magnificent limestone gorge, a dry valley between rock walls. It is renowned as home to the legendary Barguest, a spectral hound with eyes like saucers.

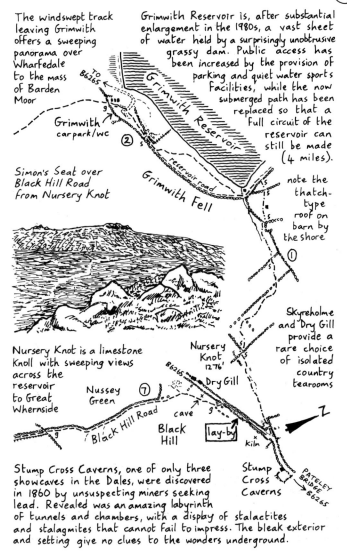

The windswept track leaving Grimwith offers a sweeping panorama over Wharfedale to the mass of Barden Moor

Grimwith Reservoir is, after substantial enlargement in the 1980s, a vast sheet of water held by a surprisingly unobtrusive grassy dam. Public access has been increased by the provision of parking and quiet water sports facilities, while the now submerged path has been replaced so that a full circuit of the reservoir can still be made (4 miles).

TO B6265

Grimwith Reservoir

Grimwith car park/wc ②

reservoir road

Grimwith Fell

note the thatch-type roof on barn by the shore

①

Simon's Seat over Black Hill Road from Nursery Knot

Skyreholme and Dry Gill provide a rare choice of isolated country tearooms

Nursery Knot is a limestone knoll with sweeping views across the reservoir to Great Whernside

Nursery Knot 1276'

B6265

Dry Gill

Nussey Green ⑦

cave

Black Hill Road

Black Hill

lay-by

kiln

N

Stump Cross Caverns, one of only three showcaves in the Dales, were discovered in 1860 by unsuspecting miners seeking lead. Revealed was an amazing labyrinth of tunnels and chambers, with a display of stalactites and stalagmites that cannot fail to impress. The bleak exterior and setting give no clues to the wonders underground.

Stump Cross Caverns

PATELEY BRIDGE B6265

3 hrs in crisp snow.
26.12.93 very nice walk

WALK 8

| AROUND THRESHFIELD MOOR |

6 miles

from Threshfield

Heather moorland
and limestone
delights combine
in the relatively
unfrequented
hinterland of
Threshfield

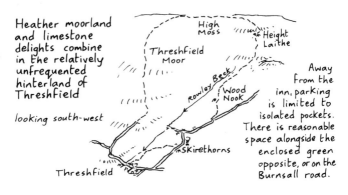

looking south-west

Away
from the
inn, parking
is limited to
isolated pockets.
There is reasonable
space alongside the
enclosed green
opposite, or on the
Burnsall road.

THE WALK

Leave the village by heading south along the main
road, over Threshfield Bridge and up the hill behind to
quickly escape by a surfaced lane on the right. Moor Lane
rises steadily to lose its surface at a junction before
continuing up to a gate onto the moor. Of the departing
tracks take the right-hand one, which curves round before
climbing steadily. As a firm track it facilitates rapid progress
up through the heather of Threshfield Moor. As a string of
stone shooting butts take shape on the left, the track is
vacated as it swings up to the right: our less discernible way
contours straight ahead, passing between the butts to run
along to an obvious wall junction ahead.

At the wall turn right to remain on the moor, and
at the first opportunity our way enters a walled section
through which it runs as a splendid green lane. At the far
end is a return to open moor, the less than dry crossing of
High Moss being aided by marker posts. On descending to a
gate limestone country is re-entered, with a much shorter
enclosed section. Before reaching a barn, the track is left
through the collapsed wall on the right, behind which a stile
precedes a wallside descent to the working barn of Height Laithe.

From a stile at the bottom, enter the yard and turn
right up a walled track. near the top turn left through a

gap and head away with the left-hand wall. Marker posts are again in evidence to guide the way to the far corner of the pasture to drop down to Height House. Passing left of the barn a stile will be located near a gate at the end of the field, and on the other side a clear path leads on to the right. This section is an absolute joy, tracing the infant Rowley Beck down through a scattered natural woodland below limestone outcrops. At the bottom a stile admits to Wood Nook caravan site, this course maintained down the drive through the site, past the house and out onto Wood Lane.

Turn down the narrow road, and at a junction keep left for Threshfield. At the next junction with a wide and dusty quarry road, escape is quickly effected by means of a stile on the right. A seldom trodden path with stiles at all the right places now leads back into Threshfield, firstly by crossing to the opposite corner, then bearing right around the bottom of two fields, a choice presents itself. The fact that Threshfield's hostelry merits its own guidepost might be sufficient incentive to follow the wall away. Crossing it part-way along, when the wall turns away rise up the field to the corner in front of the houses. A brace of stiles precede emergence alongside the Old Hall.

Threshfield is a disjointed village scattered in various directions around the junction of the Skipton to Grassington road with the main up-dale road. The 'new' part of the village - with a striking Catholic church of modern design - is along the road towards Grassington, but it is the more interesting old corner that we see. Solid stone cottages and farm buildings overlook a quaint, triangular green, enclosed by walls and shrouded in trees: spring flowers bloom inside. On turning alongside the green note the lintel of the old post office, dated 1651. The hostelry's name tells what once stood here.

The Old Hall

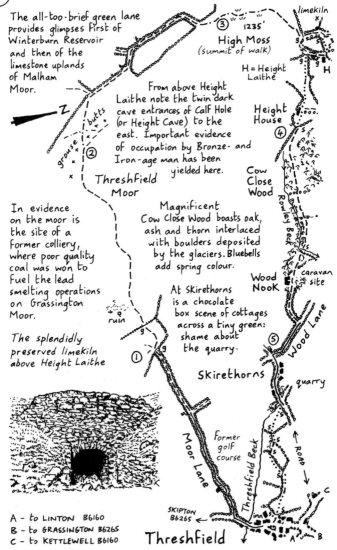

The all-too-brief green lane provides glimpses first of Winterburn Reservoir and then of the limestone uplands of Malham Moor.

limekiln

③ 1235'
High Moss
(summit of walk)

H = Height Laithe

From above Height Laithe note the twin dark cave entrances of Calf Hole (or Height Cave) to the east. Important evidence of occupation by Bronze- and Iron-age man has been yielded here.

Height House
④

grouse butts
②

Threshfield Moor

Cow Close Wood

In evidence on the moor is the site of a former colliery, where poor quality coal was won to fuel the lead smelting operations on Grassington Moor.

Magnificent Cow Close Wood boasts oak, ash and thorn interlaced with boulders deposited by the glaciers. Bluebells add spring colour.

Rowley Beck

caravan site

Wood Nook

At Skirethorns is a chocolate box scene of cottages across a tiny green: shame about the quarry.

ruin

①

The splendidly preserved limekiln above Height Laithe

⑤

Wood Lane

Skirethorns

quarry

Moor Lane

Former golf course

Threshfield Beck

Road

A – to LINTON B6160
B – to GRASSINGTON B6265
C – to KETTLEWELL B6160

SKIPTON B6265 ←

inn

Threshfield

C

A B

WALK 9 — PROVIDENCE MINES AND LANGCLIFFE EDGE

5¾ miles

from Kettlewell

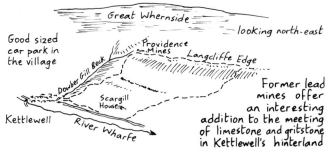

Good sized car park in the village

Great Whernside

looking north-east

Dowber Gill Beck

Providence Mines

Langcliffe Edge

Scargill House

Kettlewell

River Wharfe

Former lead mines offer an interesting addition to the meeting of limestone and gritstone in Kettlewell's hinterland

THE WALK

From the car park head into the village, and turn on the road to the right before the bridge and hotels. Fork left at the maypole to pass between the King's Head and the church and straight on along a narrow lane parallel with the beck. Just before a shapely bridge carries the road back over the beck, turn steeply up to the right on a stony bridleway.

The roughness underfoot soon gives way to an ever-improving grassy track as the gradient eases. Intervening fence and wall precede a winding course up a large pasture to reach a higher parallel wall, from where a short-lived way between crumbling walls climbs further. As one wall expires the track effects a zigzag up to the left, then crosses two virtually level pastures to the moor-gate and attendant stile.

Our route turns uphill with the wall, for a short pull to the prominent stand of cairns above long defunct Providence lead mines. From here on the route, while only a sketchy path, remains infallible as the only requirement is to accompany the wall along the well-defined Langcliffe Edge. A good mile of walking brings arrival at a ladder-stile by a gate, signalling the commencement of the return leg.

On the other side a wide panorama over Wharfedale greets the eye, and a grand track drops down, initially steeply, towards the limestone pastures. Passing through a collapsed wall the track winds down through a very long pasture, becoming indistinct but aiming for the bottom right corner. From the gate there an improving track slants down to a similar point at the edge of a plantation. Known as Highgate Leys Lane it descends the hillside, passing near Scargill House before turning left to emerge onto the Kettlewell-Conistone road.

Turn right past the drive to Scargill House, then after a couple of kinks in the narrow lane take a gate by a footpath sign on the right. Head away to a gateway then turn through it to a gate in the next wall to commence a fascinating course through about a dozen fields within half a mile. Though not visible on the ground, the way follows a near-straight wall, twice switching sides before emerging at the head of a narrow green lane on the edge of the village. Turn down it to a T-junction, and then right onto a back lane on which the walk began.

Buckden Pike from the Providence cairns

Kettlewell is the hub of the upper dale, a junction of roads and natural halting place. It stands on what was a major coaching route from London to Richmond, and the two inns at the entrance to the village would refresh many a weary traveller. The route in question still provides a tortuous way over Park Rash into Coverdale. Shops, tearooms and a third hostelry add further life to a village engulfed by holiday homes.

Kettlewell straddles its own beck, which largely drains the extensive western slopes of Great Whernside, very much Kettlewell's mountain. Some delectable cottages and gardens enviably line the beck as it races through the heart of the village to join the Wharfe, on which Kettlewell turns its back. While sheep farming clings tenuously on, the lead mining that built Kettlewell, in part, has long since been replaced by tourism as the major source of local income.

Providence Lead Mine was one of the largest in the district, and its immediate environs are littered with abandoned shafts and bell-pits. The centre of operations is found down towards Dowber Gill Beck, and our track to the moor-gate would once have been busy with loads of ore won from the mine.

The old workings - in fact the entire walk - are on the broad flanks of Great Whernside, which asserts its full stature across Dowber Gill Beck during the climb. Almost at the upper limit of the walk we witness the transition from limestone to gritstone, giving a nice change of scene for the stroll along the 1700ft contour.

The stone sentinels on the knoll above the mine mark a fine viewpoint for the mountains of the southern Dales, with Penyghent prominent.

Dowber Gill Beck

Providence Lead Mine

moor gate

Stone Men

craftsman-built from the plentiful supply of gritstone

Langcliffe Edge

Conistone Moor

N

The familiar landmark of the chapel at Scargill House blends surprisingly well into its setting. The house is a retreat and conference centre.

Scargill House

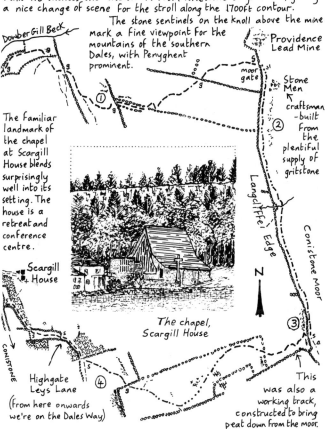

The chapel, Scargill House

CONISTONE

Highgate Leys Lane

(from here onwards we're on the Dales Way)

This was also a working track, constructed to bring peat down from the moor.

41

WALK 10

5 miles

| THROUGH STRID WOOD |

from Bolton Abbey

An outstanding
juxtaposition of
river and woodland

looking west

Large car park at
the Cavendish Pavilion,
off the road north of the village.
Alternative start: Barden Bridge (lay-by by bridge,
with riverside pasture open in season - fee payable as at Pavilion).

THE WALK

All that needs to be said is to follow one bank of
the Wharfe up to Barden Bridge, and return by the other.
There are, however, several points worthy of further comment.
From the Pavilion cross the wooden bridge and turn
upstream: shortly after entering woods the path is forced up onto
a road to negotiate Posforth Gill, but immediately returns to
the wooded bank. It clings to the river until presented with
a fork, where a simple choice is complicated by the respective
attractions of either branch. The lower path is at times an
exciting clamber over water-washed rocks, and caution is needed
if the river is high: the path runs past the Strid to eventually
meet the higher path.
Firmly recommended is this higher level option, despite its
surprisingly sustained pull to the top of the wood. Hereafter
easy walking ensues along a magnificent terrace. Although a
couple of paths later break off down to the river, the only point
of any possible doubt occurs just after the climb, keeping left
at a crossroads to pass a rest-house. On re-unification the
path leaves the wood to run past a sturdy aqueduct to arrive
at Barden Bridge.
Across the bridge a stile kicks off the return leg, soon
emerging from trees for another grassy spell past the aqueduct.
On entering Strid Wood a network of nature trail paths give
a colourful choice, though the main path is obvious throughout.
An early detour stays nearest the river to savour the High Strid
and a rock pinnacle - the Hawkstone - above the rocky path. Either
way the Strid itself, further downstream, cannot be missed, nor the
broad carriageway running back to the Cavendish Pavilion.

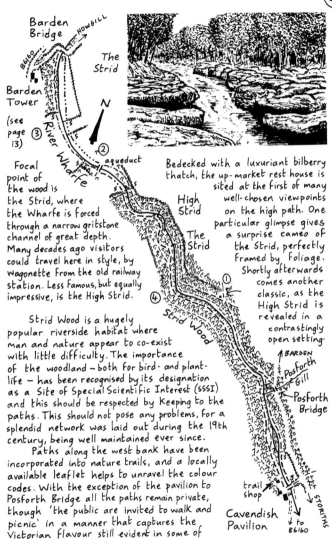

Barden Bridge

HOWGILL

B6160

The Strid

Barden Tower

(see page 13) ③

River Wharfe

N

② aqueduct

High Strid

The Strid

①

④

Strid Wood

↑BARDEN

Posforth Gill

Posforth Bridge

trail shop

Cavendish Pavilion

STORITHS

↓ to B6160

Focal point of the wood is the Strid, where the Wharfe is forced through a narrow gritstone channel of great depth. Many decades ago visitors could travel here in style, by wagonette from the old railway station. Less famous, but equally impressive, is the High Strid.

Strid Wood is a hugely popular riverside habitat where man and nature appear to co-exist with little difficulty. The importance of the woodland – both for bird- and plant-life – has been recognised by its designation as a Site of Special Scientific Interest (SSSI) and this should be respected by keeping to the paths. This should not pose any problems, for a splendid network was laid out during the 19th century, being well maintained ever since.

Paths along the west bank have been incorporated into nature trails, and a locally available leaflet helps to unravel the colour codes. With the exception of the pavilion to Posforth Bridge all the paths remain private, though 'the public are invited to walk and picnic' in a manner that captures the Victorian flavour still evident in some of the quainter touches hereabouts.

Bedecked with a luxuriant bilberry thatch, the up-market rest house is sited at the first of many well-chosen viewpoints on the high path. One particular glimpse gives a surprise cameo of the Strid, perfectly framed by foliage. Shortly afterwards comes another classic, as the High Strid is revealed in a contrastingly open setting.

WALK 11

8 miles

[ACROSS HORSE HEAD RIDGE]

from Halton Gill

A stiff
inter-valley
walk in the
heart of
the Dales.
Save it for
a clear day.

Reasonable parking, with a small lay-by opposite the green

THE WALK

Leave the green by the up-dale (Foxup) road, and beyond a bend after the last buildings take a gate on the right, curiously signposted Hawes. A broad track slopes up the field, and this same track remains our route, with little effort and no complications, to the summit of the Horse Head Pass on the broad top of this mighty ridge. The descent to the promised land of Langstrothdale is equally straightforward, the track heading directly away from the wall and soon dropping more directly and less skilfully to the bracken-clad environs of Hagg Beck. After this pleasant stretch the descent concludes at the unfenced road near Raisgill Farm.

Turn down to the left the short distance to Yockenthwaite, leave the road by the graceful bridge, and on rising to the first building turn sharp left to a gate. Here commences a magnificent ramble in the effervescent company of the infant Wharfe. After a couple of pastures the track fades as it passes Yockenthwaite Stone Circle, but from a stile beyond it a faint path materialises to rise slightly away from the river through a wall-gap to another stile. Cross the field-top to a footbridge at the other side, then on through a gap and a gate to join the access road to Deepdale. Turn down to the road and cross the uninspiring bridge to keep the road at bay.

A track sets forth up the west bank as far as lonely New House, from where a footpath continues to keep faith with the river as far as a wooden footbridge opposite the farm buildings of Beckermonds. However, our route must make its way back over the ridge, the climb beginning from a gate on the left just short of reaching the bridge and a forestry plantation.

A sketchy track starts a direct climb adjacent to a tiny beck, rising past a barn to trace the near side of the beck. When the beck acquires a distinct grassy ravine, keep above it to then follow a string of occasional, discreet cairns on a march up the fellside. At a series of shakeholes the path becomes fainter still, but once regained (note the cairn on one of the topmost boulders) is reasonably easy to follow up the higher slopes. An odd peat grough is encountered before the going eases and a well-constructed stone man on a platform is reached. The ridge-wall is now visible beyond, and a stile therein quickly gained.

On the other side the path briefly remains level, then turns sharply down to the left to pass through a long-collapsed wall and meet a level trod. Turn left along it, maintaining the contour to run past a guidepost to a ladder-stile. Remaining level a little further, and crossing over a climbing path, our path improves into a fine green way as it drops down through a modest rock gateway to a hollow above an area of limestone outcrops. From a stile in the wall ahead a sketchier continuation slants down to the far corner of the enclosure, beyond which outward steps are retraced back down into Halton Gill.

Yockenthwaite Bridge

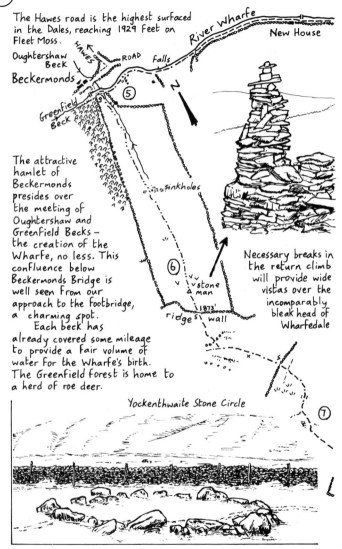

The Hawes road is the highest surfaced in the Dales, reaching 1929 feet on Fleet Moss.

HAWES ROAD

River Wharfe

New House

Oughtershaw Beck

Beckermonds

Greenfield Beck

Falls

⑤

N

The attractive hamlet of Beckermonds presides over the meeting of Oughtershaw and Greenfield Becks — the creation of the Wharfe, no less. This confluence below Beckermonds Bridge is well seen from our approach to the footbridge, a charming spot.

Each beck has already covered some mileage to provide a fair volume of water for the Wharfe's birth. The Greenfield forest is home to a herd of roe deer.

sinkholes

⑥

stone man

1873'

ridge wall

Necessary breaks in the return climb will provide wide vistas over the incomparably bleak head of Wharfedale

⑦

Yockenthwaite Stone Circle

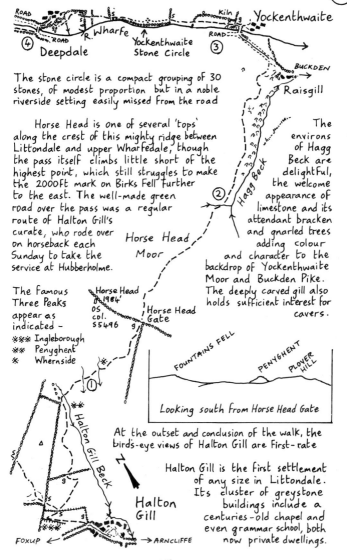

ROAD
ROAD
Kiln
Yockenthwaite
R. Wharfe
④ Deepdale
Yockenthwaite Stone Circle
③
BUCKDEN
Raisgill

The stone circle is a compact grouping of 30 stones, of modest proportion but in a noble riverside setting easily missed from the road

Horse Head is one of several 'tops' along the crest of this mighty ridge between Littondale and upper Wharfedale, though the pass itself climbs little short of the highest point, which still struggles to make the 2000ft mark on Birks Fell further to the east. The well-made green road over the pass was a regular route of Halton Gill's curate, who rode over on horseback each Sunday to take the service at Hubberholme.

The environs of Hagg Beck are delightful, the welcome appearance of limestone and its attendant bracken and gnarled trees adding colour and character to the backdrop of Yockenthwaite Moor and Buckden Pike. The deeply carved gill also holds sufficient interest for cavers.

②
Hagg Beck

Horse Head Moor

The Famous Three Peaks appear as indicated –
*** Ingleborough
** Penyghent
* Whernside

Horse Head
1984'
OS col.
SS496

Horse Head Gate

FOUNTAINS FELL   PENYGHENT   PLOVER HILL

Looking south from Horse Head Gate

①

Halton Gill Beck

N

At the outset and conclusion of the walk, the bird's-eye views of Halton Gill are first-rate.

Halton Gill is the first settlement of any size in Littondale. Its cluster of greystone buildings include a centuries-old chapel and even grammar school, both now private dwellings.

FOXUP ←   → ARNCLIFFE

Halton Gill

WALK 12

7¾ miles

MASTILES LANE AND KILNSEY MOOR

from Kilnsey

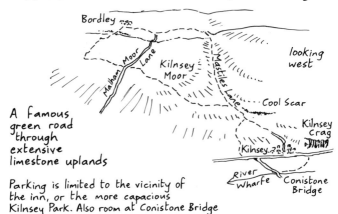

looking west

A famous green road through extensive limestone uplands

Parking is limited to the vicinity of the inn, or the more capacious Kilnsey Park. Also room at Conistone Bridge

THE WALK

Leave the main road by a side road just to the south of the Tennant Arms, climbing out of the hamlet by the forlorn ruin of the Old Hall. The road remains surfaced to approach Coolscar Quarry, but fortunately it is escaped by a more inviting track branching left before the quarry entrance. The famous Mastiles Lane now remains our chosen course for a considerable time.

Passing below the low line of Cool Scar, the old road runs unenclosed a short distance before the walls close in at a depression: on the descent thereto the road can be surveyed ahead, climbing impressively to the skyline. On eventually gaining the brow, the way drops down to Mastiles Gate, and as the road runs free again we must leave it by turning left on a grassy wallside track.

At the other end a crossroads with the terminus of a surfaced road is reached: cross straight over and head up the access road to Bordley. On the brow it becomes surfaced again to drop down to the hamlet. Just before the gate to enter its confines however, turn off left above a wall, bearing left at the end to locate a stile by a wall corner. From it climb - wallside again - the short, steep pull opposite, and at the brow keep straight on along a sketchy but fairly obvious course. The route maintains a straight line through the pasture beneath limestone scars high to the left, and soon encounters a battery of stiles set in parallel walls. From the last one aim straight ahead to a barn in the corner, where a stile deposits onto a short-lived enclosed track above Height Laithe.

Head left along the green track, which soon breaks free to cross a pasture to the Threshfield-Bordley road (Malham Moor Lane). Directly opposite another track heads off, rising gently to a minor brow before dropping to a gate in an intervening wall. Descent from Kilnsey Moor is by way of a grand track that takes a natural course through a dry, shallow valley in this vast sheep pasture.

Eventually the track winds down to the left, with a brief enclosed spell preceding rejoining Mastiles Lane. A direct return to Kilnsey simply involves retracing the first mile of the walk, but a more interesting conclusion can be enjoyed by locating a slender stile at a kink in the adjacent wall below Cool Scar. From it descend to a barn, from where an access track heads away to run steadily down to the main road.

Go left a few yards along the road before escaping along the quieter Conistone road. Just before bridging the Wharfe a stile admits to the large pasture on the left, and initially a clear track heads away. When it fades by a wall corner bear away from the river, skirting another corner en route to the prominent barn of Scar Lathe beneath the imposing wall of Kilnsey Crag itself. Here the road is rejoined, and after appraising the cliff turn left for the short walk back into Kilnsey.

On Mastiles Lane

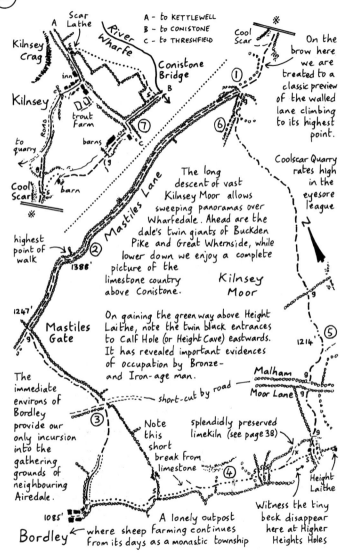

A – to KETTLEWELL
B – to CONISTONE
C – to THRESHFIELD

Scar Lathe
River Wharfe
Kilnsey Crag
Conistone Bridge
inn
Kilsney
trout Farm
barns
to quarry
barn
Cool Scar
※

Cool Scar

On the brow here we are treated to a classic preview of the walled lane climbing to its highest point.

Coolscar Quarry rates high in the eyesore league

N

highest point of walk

② 1386'

Mastiles Lane

The long descent of vast Kilnsey Moor allows sweeping panoramas over Wharfedale. Ahead are the dale's twin giants of Buckden Pike and Great Whernside, while lower down we enjoy a complete picture of the limestone country above Conistone.

Kilnsey Moor

1247'
Mastiles Gate

On gaining the green way above Height Laithe, note the twin black entrances to Calf Hole (or Height Cave) eastwards. It has revealed important evidences of occupation by Bronze- and Iron-age man.

1214

Malham Moor Lane

The immediate environs of Bordley provide our only incursion into the gathering grounds of neighbouring Airedale.

short-cut by road

③

Note this short break from limestone

splendidly preserved limekiln (see page 38)

④

Height Laithe

1085'

Bordley ← A lonely outpost where sheep farming continues from its days as a monastic township

Witness the tiny beck disappear here at Higher Heights Holes

50

Kilnsey offers attractions far outweighing its modest hamlet status. It is renowned first and foremost, of course, for the stupendous rock architecture of the Crag, whose only fault is its almost unnatural roadside location. It is a favourite climbing ground, and motorists frequently screech to a halt to weigh up the progress of rock gymnasts. After rain a clutch of springs gush exhuberantly from the base of the cliffs, whose famous overhang can brood for only one day in 365 over Kilnsey's other great draw, its show. At the back end of summer the riverside pasture across the road is alive with the colour of the dale's premier event.

As with most agricultural shows, the attractions are boosted by such long-standing Kilnsey specialities as trotting and fell-running. No prizes are offered for guessing the destination of the latter, the senior race being a major event in itself. This provides a rare chance to trespass unhindered, as in 1978 when we climbed to see the great Fred Reeves of Coniston touch the highest flag before turning for victory.

Other aspects of Kilnsey range from centuries-old hall to modern trout farm. The latter, along with the Anglers' Arms which stood almost cheek by jowl with the surviving hostelry until some decades ago, is a firm pointer to another of Kilnsey's traditions. The Old Hall, meanwhile, was built in Tudor times on the site of a grange of Fountains Abbey: today it is but a ruin.

Running up past the hall is the unspectacular start to the 'big name' in green roads of the Dales, Mastiles Lane. Riding the rolling limestone uplands, it gave access to the valuable sheep grazing grounds of Malham for the Fountains' monks, indeed continuing ultimately to their lands in Borrowdale, in Cumberland. Packmen and drovers would have taken advantage of it, though the confining walls that seem integral to its atmosphere would not have been known to its monastic patrons.

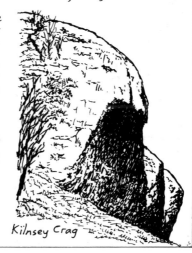

Kilnsey Crag

WALK 13

6½ miles

THE ASCENT OF SIMON'S SEAT

from Appletreewick

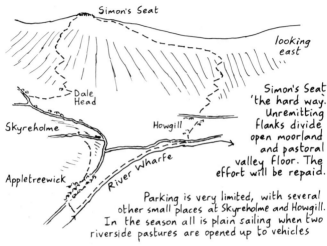

Simon's Seat
'the hard way.'
Unremitting
flanks divide
open moorland
and pastoral
valley floor. The
effort will be repaid.

Parking is very limited, with several
other small places at Skyreholme and Howgill.
In the season all is plain sailing when two
riverside pastures are opened up to vehicles

■ Between Howgill and Dale Head the walk is on Barden Fell
access area or permitted paths thereto: see foot of page 5.

THE WALK

Leave the village by the Burnsall road, past the two
inns and Low Hall to reach a walled path leading down to
the Wharfe. Turn left to commence a splendid walk down-
river the highlight being an all-too-brief wooded section.
On emerging, the path strikes across a field to meet the
narrow road at Hough Mill. Cross the adjacent bridge to
leave the road immediately in favour of a rough lane rising
to a junction at Howgill Farm.

Cross straight over to continue the climb on a track
winding up through plantations to debouch onto open moor.
The track now turns left with the wall, rising gently for a
good while before the first of several substantial cairns sets
the course for a direct strike across the moor. Soon Simon's
Seat's crown appears, and the well-trodden path reaches it
surprisingly quickly.

Having surmounted the highest rocks to attain the true summit, leave the Ordnance column and retrace steps to the gap between the main cluster of rocks and the lesser outcrops encountered first: a guidepost may be in evidence here. Turn right and within a few yards a path drops steeply to another guidepost. Ignoring the broad path left, take the more enticing one winding down through the heather. From a stile a part-sunken zigzag descent crosses the course of a pipeline, concluding through trees and bracken to emerge onto the farm road just short of Dale Head.

Go left along it as far as a gate on the right, and through it double back to a stile behind a barn. Across the next field the path goes down to a footbridge over Blands Beck and up through a yard onto the road at High Skyreholme. Go left to a junction and keep left through Skyreholme to the next junction. A quick finish is along the lane, but a better one opts for the cruel climb to the right.

Just above a barn take a stile on the left: though pathless, no further description is needed. A string of slimline gapstiles offer a fascinating conclusion, and with the cottages of Appletreewick beckoning, just keep an eye on the next stile!

Appletreewick has several claims to fame, although many visitors may best remember its delightful name. Here are three halls and two inns in amongst a wonderful assortment of cottages. All stand by the narrow road wandering through the village, from High Hall at the top - note the tiny church nearby - to Low Hall at the very bottom. Probably the oldest however is the interestingly named Mock Beggar Hall, a fine little structure once known as Monk's Hall.

Of the two hostelries one takes its name from the family of William Craven, a Dick Whittington character who found his fortune in London, becoming Lord Mayor in 1611. Not forgetting his beginnings he became a worthy local benefactor, having Burnsall's grammar school and a number of bridges in the district built.

Its fellow inn earned national fame due to the 'no-smoking' policy of a previous landlord

Simon's Seat
from the Wharfe,
Appletreewick

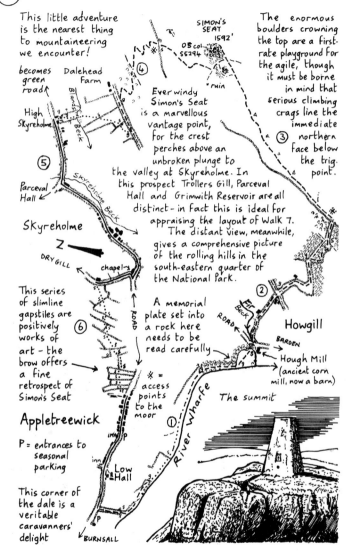

This little adventure is the nearest thing to mountaineering we encounter!

becomes green road↑ Dalehead Farm

High Skyreholme

SIMON'S SEAT 1592'

OS col. SS294

ruin

The enormous boulders crowning the top are a first-rate playground for the agile, though it must be borne in mind that serious climbing crags line the immediate northern face below the trig. point.

④

Ever windy Simon's Seat is a marvellous vantage point, for the crest perches above an unbroken plunge to the valley at Skyreholme. In this prospect Trollers Gill, Parceval Hall and Grimwith Reservoir are all distinct - in fact this is ideal for appraising the layout of Walk 7.

The distant view, meanwhile, gives a comprehensive picture of the rolling hills in the south-eastern quarter of the National Park.

⑤

Parceval Hall ←

Skyreholme

DRY GILL ←

chapel →

③

②

This series of slimline gapstiles are positively works of art - the brow offers a fine retrospect of Simon's Seat →

⑥

ROAD

A memorial plate set into a rock here needs to be read carefully

✳ = access points to the moor

Howgill

Fir

Beck

ROAD

BARDEN →

Hough Mill (ancient corn mill, now a barn)

Appletreewick

P = entrances to seasonal parking

This corner of the dale is a veritable caravanners' delight

inn

Low Hall

River Wharfe

The summit

①

↓ BURNSALL

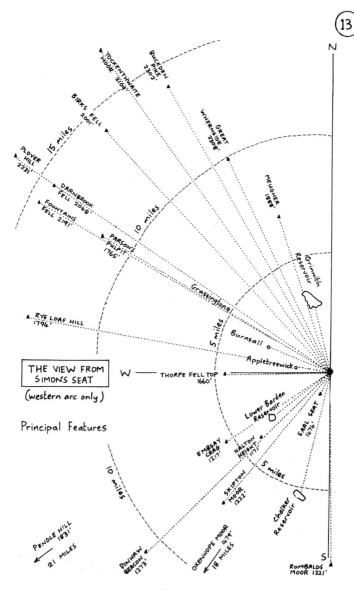

THE VIEW FROM
SIMONS SEAT

(western arc only)

Principal Features

N

13

PLOVER HILL 2231'
BIRKS FELL 2001'
YOCKENTHWAITE MOOR 2100'
BUCKDEN PIKE 2302'
GREAT WHERNSIDE 2308'
MEUGHER 1868'
DARNBROOK FELL 2048'
FOUNTAINS FELL 2191'
PARSON'S PULPIT 1765'
15 miles
10 miles
5 miles
Grimwith Reservoir
Grassington
RYE LOAF HILL 1794'
Burnsall o
Appletreewick o
W ——— THORPE FELL TOP 1660'
Lower Barden Reservoir
EARL SEAT 1474'
EMBSAY CRAG 1277'
HALTON HEIGHT 1171'
Chelker Reservoir
5 miles
SKIPTON MOOR 1222'
10 miles
PENDLE HILL 1831'
21 MILES
PINHAW BEACON 1273'
OXENHOPE MOOR 1474'
18 MILES
CHELKER Reservoir
ROMBALDS MOOR 1321'
S

55

WALK 14

2 miles

A STROLL BY THE WHARFE

from Kettlewell

The easiest walk
in the book, and
just as simple as
it looks, assuming
the river is not in flood.
Ideal for filling a spare hour.

Kettlewell — looking north-east

River Wharfe — stepping stones

Use the village car park

in Kettlewell

See also page 40

Kettlewell

BUCKDEN B6160

LEYBURN

CONISTONE

sewage works

KILNSEY B6160

R. Wharfe

Hawkswick Head Lane

'snicket' to Conistone road

also known as 'Lovers' Lane'

① stepping stones

N

THE WALK

From the car park cross the
bridge and take a stile on the left.
A path slants down to the river and
heads downstream: while for the most
part a wall of sorts keeps us off the
actual bank, towards the end the river
offers more sparkling company. A guidepost
awaits at the stepping stones, which though
bereft of character are at least dependable.

Returning dry-shod up the opposite bank, the walk
takes advantage of the leafy track known as Hawkswick Head
Lane by the untamed riverbank. When it swings away as a
snicket, a stile keeps us faithful to the Wharfe, soon passing
a sewage works and caravan site (separate!) before a final
stile takes us to the bridge, hard by the river again.

WALK 15

5¾ miles

UNDER GRASSINGTON MOOR

from Grassington

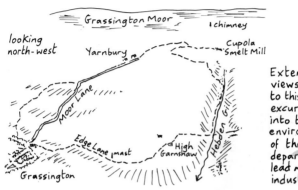

Extensive views add to this fine excursion into the environs of the departed lead mining industry

Most suitable car park is the Town Hall/Institute one, at the very top of Main Street. Alternatively, use the main Hebden Road car park.

THE WALK

At Town Head turn right along the front of the Town Hall, and take the first left along Low Lane. At the first chance leave this by a rough lane up to the left. As it levels out into a pleasant green way, take a gate on the left and follow the next wall up the field to an unobtrusive stile. From here on an indistinct path takes a diagonal course up through a succession of fields to emerge by a gate onto Edge Lane.

Turning right along it, the walled lane improves into a splendid green way, passing a tall mast before entering a tract of open moor. The track slants up to the left with expanding views across Hebden Gill before the walls close in again. The surprise of seeing a farm (New House) ahead is doubled by the appearance of another, High Garnshaw, in the dip just below. The walled lane (Tinkers' Lane) runs past the latter then climbs close to the former. On it continues, open then enclosed, to drop down to the floor of Hebden Gill.

Turning up the beckside, the track runs through old

lead mining remains. At a limekiln the track turns up to the left, climbing through more spoil heaps to a junction with the broad track known as the Duke's New Road. Across to the left is an area of several interesting mining features including the Beever Dam, while the main track bears left, aiming directly for Yarnbury past a row of bell-pits. Turning right, however, the Duke's New Road contours around to approach Cupola Smelt Mill. Refer to the notes opposite regarding exploration beyond this point.

Returning a few yards along the 'road' to cross the infant beck, branch off to the right to locate a stile in a bend in the wall. Here Old Moor Lane is joined, and followed left to become surfaced at Yarnbury. This traffic-free road, now known simply as Moor Lane, continues all the way down into Grassington. Before the road starts a more purposeful drop, the conclusion can be improved upon by taking up the offer of a stile on the right: after crossing a field the route descends steeply to the head of a green lane, following it down to a short-lived snicket and then going left along Chapel Street back to the start.

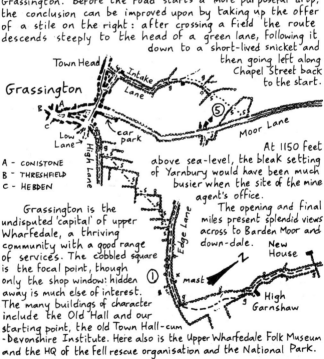

A – CONISTONE
B – THRESHFIELD
C – HEBDEN

At 1150 feet above sea-level, the bleak setting of Yarnbury would have been much busier when the site of the mine agent's office.

Grassington is the undisputed 'capital' of upper Wharfedale, a thriving community with a good range of services. The cobbled square is the focal point, though only the shop window: hidden away is much else of interest. The many buildings of character include the Old Hall and our starting point, the old Town Hall-cum-Devonshire Institute. Here also is the Upper Wharfedale Folk Museum and the HQ of the fell rescue organisation and the National Park.

The opening and final miles present splendid views across to Barden Moor and down-dale.

Grassington Moor was one of the major centres of lead mining in the Yorkshire Dales, and along with the Pateley Bridge area rivalled activities in Swaledale. Though dating back to Roman times, the industry reached its peak in the early 19th century, and ended completely before the end of that century.

Features near our route include:-

- Beever Dam - served a crushing mill and pump and winding gear in Union Shaft
- Union Shaft - 360ft deep (covered shaft!) drained into Hebden Gill by Duke's Level
- Cupola Smelt Mill - built 1793 by Duke of Devonshire (of course). Fired by local coal
- Flues - a one-mile system taking fumes from mill to chimney (via condensors)
- chimney - at top of flue system, saved and preserved 1971 by indefatigable Earby Mines Research Group

Cupola Flue and chimney

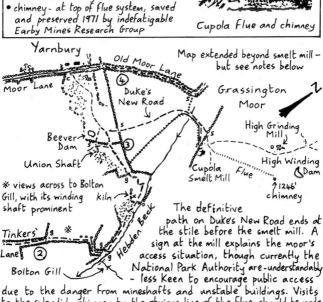

Yarnbury

Old Moor Lane

Map extended beyond smelt mill - but see notes below

Moor Lane

④ Duke's New Road ↓

Grassington Moor

High Grinding Mill

Beever Dam

③

Union Shaft

Cupola Smelt Mill

Flue

High Winding Dam

✳ views across to Bolton Gill, with its winding shaft prominent

kiln

1246' chimney

Tinkers' Lane

② ✳

Bolton Gill

Hebden Beck

The definitive path on Duke's New Road ends at the stile before the smelt mill. A sign at the mill explains the moor's access situation, though currently the National Park Authority are - understandably - less keen to encourage public access due to the danger from mineshafts and unstable buildings. Visits to the splendid chimney by the obvious line of the Flue should be made alongside the flue, and not on it!

WALK 16

3½ miles

LANGSTROTHDALE

from Hubberholme

Very easy walking in the unspoilt and ravishingly beautiful environs of the infant Wharfe

Parking is limited to the riverside by the church, or for patrons, the car park of the George. Alternatively, use the roadside verge updale of Yockenthwaite Bridge.

THE WALK

Leave Hubberholme by a gate adjacent to the church, from where a broad drive climbs to isolated Scar House. Passing between the buildings, turn left at the top to a stile by a gate, from where a sketchy path sets an obvious course through the minor outcrops of a limestone shelf.

Through a small wood the path crosses over the ravine of Strans Gill, then slants half-left before maintaining a level traverse through numerous walls in various conditions. Further on, it is diverted to slant down to a wall before running on through more trees to emerge on a scarred track above Yockenthwaite.

The track drops down to the farming hamlet, and without crossing the shapely bridge our return route doubles back down to a gate above the river. Quickly on the bank of the Wharfe no further instructions need be given, the path shadowing the river back to Hubberholme, and emerging onto the outward track behind the church.

Yockenthwaite was named 'Eogan's clearing' by Norsemen who settled here. Its graceful bridge leads to cottages and farms that once formed a community that supported both inn and school, and no doubt before that, the hunting Forest.

Though barely even a hamlet, Hubberholme boasts two famous buildings and a shapely bridge which connects them. The church of St. Michael is a gem, with its tower showing Norman traces. Its best feature is a 500-year old oak rood loft, one of only two remaining in Yorkshire, while some pews bear the famous trademark of 'Mousey' Thompson. Outside, meanwhile, the sparkling Wharfe runs almost past its very door.

Across the river is the whitewashed and homely George Inn in an idyllic setting. Formerly housing the vicar, its flagged floors continued to be the scene of the New Year 'land-letting', when the proceeds from a poor pasture go to the needy parishioners.

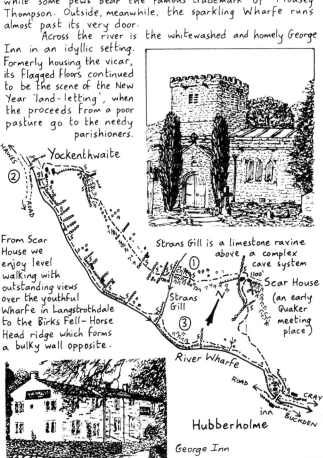

Yockenthwaite

HAWES ROAD

②

From Scar House we enjoy level walking with outstanding views over the youthful Wharfe in Langstrothdale to the Birks Fell - Horse Head ridge which forms a bulky wall opposite.

Strans Gill is a limestone ravine above a complex cave system

①

Strans Gill

③

Scar House (an early Quaker meeting place)

1100'

River Wharfe

ROAD

CRAY

BUCKDEN

inn

Hubberholme

George Inn

LOG OF THE WALKS

These two pages provide an opportunity to maintain
a permanent record of the walks completed

WALK	DATE	TIME Start	Finish	WEATHER	COMMENTS	
1						
2						
3						
4						
5						
6						
7						
8						

WALK	DATE	TIME Start	TIME Finish	WEATHER	COMMENTS		
9							
10							
11							
12							
13							
14							
15							
16							

KEY TO THE MAP SYMBOLS

direction of north

scale
2½ inches = 1 mile (approx)

Route — clear — sketchy — no visible path

Route on public road — unenclosed — wall — fence/hedge

River/beck — bridge

Marsh

Peat grough

Crags

Limestone clints

Loose rocks/ scree

Cairns
summit   other

Trees

Buildings

Church

Abbreviations
c = cattle grid
s = stile
g = gate

Miles from start
③

THE COUNTRY CODE

Respect the life and work of the countryside
Protect wildlife, plants and trees
Keep to public paths across farmland
Safeguard water supplies
Go carefully on country roads
Keep dogs under control
Guard against all risks of fire
Fasten all gates
Leave no litter - take it with you
Make no unnecessary noise
Leave livestock, crops and machinery alone
Use gates and stiles to cross fences, hedges and walls